Christmas Prayers

by
Judith Hannemann

authorHOUSE®

AuthorHouse™
1663 Liberty Drive
Bloomington, IN 47403
www.authorhouse.com
Phone: 1-800-839-8640

First published by AuthorHouse   12/02/2010
ISBN: 978-1-4520-8125-0 (sc)
ISBN: 978-1-4520-8126-7 (e)
Library of Congress Control Number: 2010918140

Printed in the United States of America

This book is printed on acid-free paper.

Dedication

For Jake, in gratitude for his Christmas
gifts of love and prayer.

For the Reader

May your Christmas be blessed by the appearance of the Lord Jesus in your heart.

May His grace sustain you and your loved ones in celebration of His Birth.

May He sit at your holiday table, decorate your home with joy, open with you the gift of His great love for you.

May the wonder of His Presence remain with you long after the last ornament and ribbon are packed away.

May His Holy Spirit of Grace and Supplication anoint your prayers every day of the New Year.

And may you receive the prayers of this book as my greeting for a Holy Christmas

Amen.

Advents

Blessed Lord Jesus,

Two Advents approach.

One Advent on a liturgical calendar. Three purple and one rose candle in a wreath of greens.

Scripture readings; purple vestments and altar hangings. Anticipation in the church.

The other Advent a preparation spoken by You in parable.

Ten bridesmaids drowsing in denial. Unexpected arrival of the groom.

Mercifully fill our hearts with the oil of Your Holy Spirit that our lamps might be in readiness to greet Your Second Coming.

In Your unending goodness, keep us as alert to the eternal Advent as we are to the liturgical Advent.

Ignite our faith to be in readiness and rejoicing for both Advents.

Astonish us with the grace to be a people as prepared for the Babe as for the Bridegroom

Thank You, Lord.

Amen.
Matt. 25:1-13(RSV)

Waiting

Heavenly Father,

Mercifully expand Your grace to us in our waiting for the appearance of our great God and Savior Jesus Christ.

We have great need of Your divine help if we are to be a people purified for Christ Jesus.

Our waiting for His appearance is tempted by heart detours.

The world with its passions waits for us on television channels,in magazine articles, web-sites; waits for us in Malls, store aisles and restaurants; waits for us in holiday socializing; waits for us in pretense and exhaustion.

Hear the desire of our hearts for a Holy Advent.

Sweeten our waiting with the Presence of Your Holy Spirit.

We would be a people of prepared hearts wherein the Bethlehem Babe can cradle.

Thank You, Father.

Amen.
Titus 2:11-14

Errands

Beloved friend of faith,

May your Christmas footsteps, wherever they take you, for whatever their cause, be holy in the company of the Lord Jesus because Your Lord delights in you.Psalm37:23.

May you realize every step you take is guarded by God's love for you.1 Samuel 2:9.

May your spirit be aware of the holy angels who are given charge of you lest you stumble. Psalm 91;11.

May you walk in the Light of Christ and project His Light into all your personal encounters.1John 1:7.

May the hearts and the paths of the persons you love and pray for at Christmas be illuminated by the Light of Christ's love in you.

May your footsteps on Christmas errands be blessed by this prayer. And may you remember to pray for me.

Amen.

A Listening Christmas

…whoever listens to me will live in safety and be at ease
without fear of harm.

Prov. 1:33(NIV)

Dear one in the faith,

At this time of gift giving, may the Lord Jesus' gift to
you be a listening ear that you might be safe, at ease and
unafraid.

A listening ear to hear God's singing of His great love
for you.

A listening ear to hear the heart cries of the people He
has placed in your life.

A listening ear to hear His travel directions to
Bethlehem.

A listening ear to be silent in spirit as He speaks into
your life.

A listening ear to accept and to be obedient to His will
for your life.

A listening ear to have an eternal perspective of the
darkness and the conflict of the world.

A listening ear to recognize and follow the Divine
Shepherd's voice.

Be blessed by this prayer for a listening Christmas, and
likewise please pray for me to listen.

Amen.

Awakening

Blessed is he who is awake when he comes;
Luke 12:37(RSV)

Dear Friend in Faith,

May the Lord Jesus awaken your heart every morning of Advent and the Twelve Days of Christmas.

Awaken your soul to His call and not to the alarm clock of the world's urgencies.

Awaken your tired limbs to serve and to share the Manger Miracle.

Awaken your life to accept His will for you.

Awaken your spirit to accept the gift of His love for you.

Awaken your mind to apprehend and embrace the Messianic prophecies.

Awaken your feet to follow Him into stores, parties and Post Offices.

Awaken your opportunities to witness to His saving mercy.

Awaken your heart to pray for me as I do for you.

May you and I be blessed every morning by awakening to the True Light of Christmas, our Lord and Savior, Jesus Christ.

May He be our strength every morning.

Amen.
Is.32:2(RSV)

Christmas Thanks

With joy you will draw water from the wells
of salvation. And you will say in that day:
"Give thanks to the Lord,
call upon His name;
make known His deeds among the nations,
proclaim His name is exalted."

Isaiah 12:3-4 (RSV)

Lord Jesus Christ, Living Water,
 When we read…"the birth of Jesus took place in this
way"(Mt.1:18),our childlike hearts remember and realize
anew the reason for Christmas.
 We may draw You from the wells of salvation.
 Grant to us the gift of thankful hearts this Christmas.
 Thankful for the loved ones left to us in this life.
 Thankful for the departed ones who are home with You
this Christmas.
 Thankful for the season honoring Your birth.
 Thankful for holiday opportunities to share the reason
for Christmas.
 Thankful for Your helping us travel from preparations
and preoccupations to Your Manger.
 Thankful for wisdom to proclaim Your salvation to
fellow travelers.
 Thankful for Your saturating our hearts with Your Holy
Spirit .
 Thankful for the joy of You in our Christmas.

Amen.

Areopagus

… I perceive in every way you are very religious…
Acts 11:22

Blessed Lord Jesus, Lord of Christmas,

Mercifully hear the cry of our hearts for wisdom and for witness during the holiday season. Our sensibilities are assaulted by foreign gods.

Altars "To an Unknown God" are on the counters and in the kiosks of the Mall.

Glittering wreaths, sparkling tree ornaments, pillars of cranberry scented candles.

Cookies, candy canes, gingerbread houses, red and green jelly beans.

Christmas greeting cards, gift bags, wrapping paper, ribbons, bows and tags, stocking stuffers, New Year calendars. Bowls and platters painted with Santas, reindeer and snowmen. Wines, beers, gourmet hams, cakes.

Crimson table cloths and holly shaped napkin rings.

Poinsettias, paper-whites, garlands of greenery, topiary trees.

Red ties and vests for men, holiday motif sweaters for women, elf pajamas, velour bathrobes.

Shoppers and salesclerks unaware that in You we live and move and have our being.

The liturgy of shopping, accompanied by a choral cacophony of "Jingle Bells."

Mercifully extend Your grace to enhance our speech and gestures that we might witness to You, the Eternal One, Immanuel.

Lord of Christmas, go with us to the Areopagus.

Amen.

Company for Christmas

We wait in hope for the Lord.
Psalm 33:20-22(NIV)

Lord Jesus,
Image of the Invisible God.
Babe of Bethlehem.
Divine Traveler to us at Christmas.
Incarnate Visitor from Heaven,

You travel to us through time without a ticket, a
boarding pass or security check.
Your reservation originated in the heart of God before
all time. Your ETA not of our design, but determined by
the Father. Knowing You did not need to check luggage, He
made Your travel arrangements. Your arrival announced on
the heavenly intercom by multitudes of Heavenly Host.
We await You at the gate of Your appearing.
We have prepared a guest room of our hearts.
We rejoice at Your arrival, for we trust in Your Holy Name.

Son of Mary.
Holy One of God.
Lord of Glory.
Power of God.
Star out of Jacob.

May Your unfailing love rest upon us as we welcome You
this Christmas .

Amen.

Bed and Breakfast

There is plenty of room for you in my Father's home. If that were not so, would I have told you that I'm on my way to get a room ready for you ? And if I'm on my way to get a room ready, I'll come back and get you so you can live where I live.

John 14:3-4 (The Message)

Beloved Traveler in the foreign land of illness,

Should this Christmas be your last celebration with loved ones, know a holy bed and breakfast await you.

Know the Lord Jesus has prepared a room for you in His Father's home.

The Holy Angels have put fresh sheets on your bed, swept the floor, washed the windows to admit the Light of eternity.

His Holy Spirit has tidied the closets so no sin can hang there. Your traveling clothes, so smirched by struggle and sin, have been washed in the blood of the Lamb. Your bath water is drawn; clean towels are ready. All that held or hurt you on earth will be washed away.

A meal of The Bread of Life awaits you. He has said He wants you to be where He is.

Believe the Lord Jesus will come back and get you when your guest room in eternity is ready.

Amen .

Christmas Doors

Behold I stand at the door and knock; if any man hears
my voice and opens the door, I will come in to him and
will eat with him, and he with me.

Rev.3:20(NIV)

Lord Jesus,

Every door along the street is decorated for Christmas.
Spruce wreaths with scarlet bows , reindeer sleds, candy
canes, laughing Santa Claus faces.

Colorful Christmas decor to welcome guests.

In Your mercy, help us turn down the worldly electronic
volume, chatter, traffic sounds and even Christmas carols to
hear Your knocking at the doors of our hearts .Courteous as
You are, You knock and wait and do not force the door.

Help us summon the courage to open the door to You
where You wait on the porch of our lives.

Come into our hearts and our homes. Such food
preparation there is for the holiday. Cupboards and cookie
jars and refrigerators filled with treats when You alone, the
Bread come down from Heaven, satisfies our hunger.

Sit at our tables. Feed our hearts .

Satisfy us with Your Holiday Presence.

Thank You for being our Divine Dinner Guest this
Christmas.

Amen.

A Gabriel Christmas

For with God, nothing is impossible.
Luke 1:37(RSV)

Almighty God,
No Word from You is without power and possibility.

Our hearts beseech You for a Gabriel Christmas of fully apprehending Your Word.

Mercifully teach us to embrace Your Divine Power as we pray for the seemingly "impossibles":

- ❖ Conversion this Christmas of our family members who live outside the Kingdom
- ❖ Healing for dear friends who are ill, especially those with cancer who celebrate their last Christmas
- ❖ Bereaved friends whose hearts are heavy at the holidays
- ❖ Revival of faith in the USA and a return to being "one nation under God"
- ❖ Protection from violence and a return to lawfulness
- ❖ The hearts of persons without love to be filled with God's love for them this Christmas
- ❖ Food, shelter and the mercy of kindness and care for the homeless, the impoverished ,the addicted
- ❖ Our deployed military and their families be blessed and strengthened
- ❖ The Prince of Peace to be revealed to the nations of the world.
- ❖ Hear from Heaven and answer our prayers, offered in the Name of Your Son, the Lord Jesus Christ.

Amen.

Christmas Music

Sing and make music in your heart to the Lord,
always giving thanks to God the Father for everything,
in the Name of our Lord Jesus Christ.
Eph 5:19(b)-20(NIV)

May He who makes all things new put a new song in your
heart.

May its newness revitalize your holiday celebration with
love for your Savior.

May its rhythm refresh your wonder at the Word made
flesh, the Babe of Bethlehem.

May its harmony accompany you in all your
preparations and prompt you to share the Miracle with all
persons you encounter.

May its lyrics be of thankfulness for your Salvation and
for everything in your life.

May every Christmas carol you hear be an echo of the
joyful angelic chorus over Bethlehem.

May your Christmas be blessed with "songs to the Lord"
in your heart.

In the Name of our Lord Jesus Christ, I bid you sing!

Amen.

Refiner's Fire

> But who can endure the day of His coming?
> Who can stand when He appears?
> For He will be like a refiner's fire...
>> Mal. 3:2(NIV)

Blessed Holy Spirit, Fire of God,

Purify our hearts for the approaching birthday of the Lord Jesus.

We are caught unprepared by the rapid passage of clock and of calendar time.

Purify us for His appearing.

Separate us from the extraneous dross of the world.

Distill our dullness of spirit.

By Your Holy Energy, burn away the alloy of regrets and failures to forgive.

Fire of God, ignite our holiday hearts with passion and purpose for our Lord Jesus.

Refiner's Fire, reduce us to a pure and refined state of joy in Jesus Christ, whose burning witness you are.

Amen.

Bethlehem Blessing for the Reader

"Let us go over to Bethlehem and see this thing that has happened, which the Lord has made known to us."
Luke 2:15(RSV)

May the Holy Spirit travel with you to Bethlehem.

May you have the spiritual strength to avoid distractions, detours, delays.

May the Babe of Bethlehem be born anew in your heart.

May the wonder and the joy of His Nativity be refreshed for you.

May the prayers herein help your travel.

And may you return from Bethlehem as did the shepherds, "… glorifying and praising God for all they had heard and seen, as it had been told to them."(Luke 2:20(RSV).

Amen.

Holiday Spirit

Meanwhile, the moment we get tired in the waiting,
God's Spirit is right alongside helping us along.
If we don't know how or what to pray, it doesn't matter.
He does our praying in and for us.
Rom.8:26-27(The Message)

Holy Spirit of God,
Thank You for refreshing us in the waiting.
Cash register line waiting; Post Office line waiting;
Traffic light waiting; Package delivery waiting.
Advent waiting for the Birthday Party of the Lord Jesus.
Waiting for the most essential; for all creation to be
revealed in eternity.
Thank You for being right alongside us, helping us sort out
secular celebration from the wonder of the Word made Flesh.
Thank You for doing our praying when we do not know
how to pray for a holy Christmas.
Thank You for praying in us for our loved ones,
especially those who are not yet in the Kingdom.
Thank You for keeping us present before God.
Thank You for coming alongside us as the flowering and
the flame of faith in Christ Jesus.
Thank You for traveling with us to Bethlehem.
Spirit of Grace and Supplication.
Breath of Life.
Holy Spirit of God.
Thank You for Your Christmas Companionship.

Amen.

Children

The children were brought to Him that He might lay
His hands on them and pray.
Matt 19:13(RSV)

Lord Jesus,

In Your mercy, lay Your hands upon the child within us
as we await Christmas.

We are much consumed with the adult idols of
Christmas. Idols in store windows and clothing racks. Idols
in ritual parties and gift exchanges. Idols in decoration and
expenditure.

We would be Your children. Children of Christmas.

We long for the glowing expectancy of children's
eyes. Expectancy for a magical morning of dolls, legos,
skateboards.

Our magical morning is in a manger that promises an
empty tomb and eternity.

Fill our hearts and our eyes with the glowing expectancy
of Your Nativity. Gather us into Your Divine arms where we
are safe from idols.

We long for the heart of a child as we await celebration
of Your birth.

Lay Your hands upon the child we would be and pray for us.

Thank You for always praying for us at the right hand of
The Father.

Amen.

Holy Shepherd

I myself will tend my sheep and have them
lie down, says the Sovereign Lord.
Ezek. 34:15(NIV)

Sovereign Lord,
   In Your great love, come to us at Christmas.
Our hearts and our holidays have great need of You.
   Come to us, Holy Shepherd.
   Search us out in our stumbling celebrations of self.
   Seek us out in our beribboned and glittered scattering of
attention away from You.
   Stabilize us against our weakness for secular festivity.
   Grant to Your flock the blessed peace and comfort of the
sheep who were lying in the fields of Bethlehem when the
announcing angel appeared to the shepherds.
   Secure. Content. Protected.
   Our drowsing eyelids opened and filled with the glory of
God shinning all around.
   Healed and held.
   Searched and sought after.
   Cossets of Your grace.
   Come to us at Christmas.

Amen.

Christmas Grief

He was despised and rejected by men.
…a man of sorrows, and acquainted with grief.
Surely he has borne our griefs and carried our sorrows.
Isaiah 53:3b & 4(RSV)

Dear one who grieves at Christmas,

Know that the Lord Jesus shares your grief this Christmas.

He was at the hospital bedside of your loved one, sitting quietly in mystical union, holding out His nail-scarred hand of welcome to eternity.

He was present at the wake and the visiting hours, present with you at the funeral, carrying your sorrow in His broken heart.

As He stood with you beside the grave, His Divine tears fell upon the casket with yours.

He is in the closet of clothing and the dresser drawers of personal affects to be bundled away.

He is present beside your Christmas tree, to celebrate and decorate, when no Christmas can ever be the same again.

He is now present at your holiday dinner table, sitting in the empty chair and in your empty heart.

Feast upon His Love for you, dear one who grieves at Christmas.

Amen.

The Star

"Where is He who has been born king of the Jews?
For we have seen his star in the East and have come
to worship him".

Matt. 2:2(RSV)

Gold. Frankincense, Myrrh.
They fell down and worshiped You.
Our hearts. Our harried holidays. Our lives.
They are the only treasures we have to lay beside Your
manger cradle.
We also fall down and worship You.
Power of God.
The Lord from Heaven.
The Christ of God.
King of the Ages.
The Holy One of God.
The Gift of God.
Lord of All.
Beloved Son of God.
Son of the Most High.
Son of Mary.
In Your mercy, receive our worship as our gift of love
and of gratitude for coming to us in our flesh.
We have seen Your Star and the brightness of Your
rising. Strengthen us to share You with family, friends and
passers-by who remain in darkness.
Bless our Christmas and theirs with the joy of seeing the
star in the East and following it to You.

Amen.

House Blessing

I will cause my people and their homes around
my holy hill to be a blessing. And I will send showers,
showers of blessings, which will come just when they are
needed.

Ezek. 34:26(NLT)

Sovereign Lord,

In Your great mercy, establish our homes and our hearts
as blessings.

Our Jerusalem, our holy hill, is of the heart until
eternity.

We ask for showers of blessings in articulating the
Incarnation of Your Son.

Bless our homes as holy hospitality to our family and
friends.

Bless our speech as affirmation of Your grace.

Bless our meals as feasts welcoming Jesus, our Divine
Guest.

We would be a people of blessings to others and can but
entreat Your Christmas Blessings on our attempts.

Bless us, Your people, with the greatest of all blessings,
the Christmas Presence of Your Son, the Lord Jesus Christ,
in Whose Name we pray.

Amen.

Golden Bowl

…and the twenty-four elders fell down before the Lamb,
each holding a harp, and with a golden bowl full of
incense, which are the prayers of the saints.

Rev. 5:8,b(RSV)

Dear Pilgrim in Prayer,

Thank you for sharing with me this journey in prayer.

May you be refreshed in your travel towards the heart of
God.

May you be encouraged to pray by remembering your
prayers, even troubled and confused prayers, are incense to
the Lamb.

None are wasted; none will remain unanswered; none
are forgotten by the Lamb.

May the lifting up of your hands and your heart be like
the evening sacrifice, a pleasing aroma to the Lord Jesus,
Whose heart contains them into eternity.

When you pray, may your refreshed voice of praise join
the voices of the living creatures and elders, the myriads and
thousands of angels, singing a new song:

"To Him who sits upon the throne, and to the Lamb
be blessing and honor and glory and might forever and
ever!Amen.," (v.11-14)

Amen.

Christmas Heart Peace

Let me hear what God the Lord will speak, for He will
speak peace to His people,
to His saints, to those who turn to Him in their hearts.
Psalm 85:8(RSV)

Lord Jesus, Prince of Peace,
Be our peace this Christmas. Speak to us in the tinseled
tasks of holiday urgencies. Your people, Your saints, long for
the heart peace sung by multitudes of Heavenly Host over
Bethlehem.

Speak to us amid news of war in the Middle East,
terrorism threats, unemployment, economic instability,,
corporate and individual corruption, flu epidemics, cancer
statistics, crime rates, violence.

Speak to us of Your peace that comforts grief, heals
illness, brings hope.

Speak to us of Your eternal peace as we struggle with our
ephemeral existence.

Speak to us of the paradox of You as King of Kings,
born in a stable, staggering under a Cross to Your Throne.

We turn to You in our hearts.

Lord Jesus, Prince of Peace, be our peace this Christmas.

Amen.

Highway

A voice of one calling, "In the desert prepare the way of the Lord; make straight in the wilderness a highway for our God."

Isaiah 40:3-5(NIV)

May you be anointed to make straight in the wilderness a highway to our God.

Wilderness of shopping malls and ritual office and neighborhood parties.

Wilderness of secular celebrations and TV commercials.

Wilderness of Christmas without Christ.

May you have the eyes of faith to see the road disrepair of all persons you encounter.

Travel delays of pride, anger, unforgiveness.

Ruts of deaths, illness, loss, abandonment.

Detours of worldly distractions into the wilderness.

May the pavement of your prayers begin road construction for the Lord's travel.

May the Holy Spirit equip you with words of witness to begin the repair work.

May King Jesus travel without road blocks to the hearts of all these persons.

And may your Christmas and theirs be blessed with the Love and the Power of His Presence.

Merry Christmas.

Amen.

Grief Bearer

Surely He has borne our griefs,
and carried our sorrows.
Is.53:4(RSV)

Lord Jesus,

We carry packages to the Post Office, sacks of groceries to the car, a fresh Christmas tree to the living room. We carry cookies as gifts, wine bottles of holiday cheer, snow shovels and sleds to the garage.

Our packages heavy for us; Your packages even heavier and not seasonal.

You carried our griefs and our sorrows on the Cross.

And You continue to carry them, ever interceding for us at the right hand of the Father.

You carry our griefs for lost loved ones, holiday haunting from Christmases past, disappointments, defections and disenchantments.

Our griefs are plural; Your carrying is singular; once and for all time on the Cross for all mankind.

Thank You, Man of Sorrows, for carrying our sins on the Cross.

Grief Bearer, mercifully remind us this Christmas that You carry us. Thank You, Lord.

Amen.

Christmas Rose

In that day the Root of Jesse will stand as a banner,
for the peoples; the nations will rally to him,
and his place of rest will be glorious.
Is.11:10(NIV)

Rose of Sharon, Lord Jesus Christ,
Bloom in us this Christmas.
Bloom amid the cold of winter and the coldness of our
hearts, unaware and distracted as they are.
Bloom as the flourishing of faith in doubts.
Bloom as the fragrance of mercy in relationships,
Bloom as the flowering of gratitude for salvation.
Florescence of God, bloom in us as witnesses to
Your Banner of grace.
Rose of Sharon.
Son of David.
Most Tender Shoot.
Blossoming Root of Jesse.
Messiah.
Bloom in us this Christmas.

Amen.

Christmas Root

Of this man's posterity (David, the son of Jesse)
God has brought to Israel, a Savior, Jesus, as He
promised.

Acts 13:23(RSV)

Root of Jesse,

In this Scripture, we see two shepherds and two kings.
One a young boy waiting to be called to kill Goliath, waiting
for his destiny as an earthly king.

The other an Eternal Shepherd calling His own, called
to kill sin by His own death, a Heavenly King waiting for us
in eternity.

Righteous branch, from Whom all mercy sprouts,
strengthen us with a growth of Your grace this Christmas.

The trees and bushes of December are without foliage,
yet our hearts desire the green-ness of Your grace.

Call to us anew that we might hear Your voice and
follow.

Blossom within us in goodness and generosity to the
persons You have placed in our lives.

Replace the holiday hurry with a holy time, a time of
celebration rooted in You,

Thank You, Root of Jesse.

Amen.

Gift Wrap

The grace of God has appeared for the salvation of all
men…

Titus 2:11(TSV)

Blessed Lord Jesus,

In this season of purchasing, wrapping and mailing
gifts, appear to us.

Appear to us as we wait in long tiring cash register and
Post Office lines.

Appear to us in the covering of gift boxes with
picturesque paper depicting angels and reindeer, in tying red
and green ribbons and fashioning bows, in filling out gift
tags.

Appear in our hearts this Christmas, we beseech You.

By Your appearance, mercifully deflect our focus away
from frenetic festivity to receive the grace of God, our
salvation.

You are the most precious Gift of God to us. His Holy
Name is on the gift tag.

We untie the ribbon of mercy, remove the gift wrap of
forgiveness, lift the lid of the Father's love and find You,
Jesus, the True Gift of Christmas.

Beautiful Babe of Bethlehem, inspire and energize our
gift giving to share Your message with all men and women
we encounter in our holiday preparation.

Amen.

True Light

There was a man sent from God, whose name was John.
He came for testimony, to bear witness to the
light that all might believe through him. He was not
the light. The true light that enlightens every man was
coming into the world.

John 1:6-8(RSV)

Lord Jesus Christ, True Light,
   Come to us in Holy Illumination.
   You are the True Light, not manufactured in China nor
purchased at Wal-Mart to brighten our holiday.
   Reveal to us the meaning of the True Light that alone
gives life to men.
   Shine into our individual darkness of sin and self; shine
into our collective social darkness of violence and nihilism.
   Mercifully hear and answer our desire to be a witness to
the Light You are.
   Blessed Light.
   True Light.
   Incandescence of God.
   Holy Light.
   Light to the Nations.
   Leading Light.
   Scrutinizing Light.
   Life Giving Light.
   Light the darkness has not overcome.
   Come to us, Lord Jesus, in Holy Illumination.

Amen.

A Quiet Place

Then because so many people were coming and going and they had not even had a chance to eat, He said to them, "Come with me by yourselves to a quiet place and get some rest."

Mark 6:31 (RSV)

Lord Jesus,

You call to us in the constant holiday coming and going of people in our lives. Appointments; phone calls; planning celebrations; deliveries; questions; TV urgencies; overhead airplanes; auto entry beeps; snow plows; ambulance sirens; honking cars; cell phone chatter; 50MPH.

You know we have not even had a chance to eat of You, the Bread come down from Heaven, the food which alone gives nourishment.

Through the most generous guidance of Your Holy Spirit, help us come away by ourselves to a quiet place with You during the Christmas season.

Help us hear Your calling us to rest in You, to discover within ourselves the inner heart of quiet listening to You.

Feed us with Your Presence, O Lord of Christmas.

Amen.

Christmas Trees of Healing

He was bruised for our iniquities;
upon him was the chastisement that made us whole,
and with his stripes we are healed.
Is.53:5 (NIV)

Lord Jesus,

The Christmas tree lights are blue, red and yellow,
the ornaments a precious collection from years of family
tradition, the tinsel glitters against an array of tiny angels,
stars and candy canes.

Our symbol of Your Birthday. The Christmas Tree.

Another tree looms in paradox. The Cross.

Blessed Jesus, Man of sorrows, one acquainted with
grief, thank You for carrying our sorrows.

We bring to Your Manger and to Your Cross our grief
for our dear lost ones, our illnesses and pains, our failures
and our transgressions.

Beside our Christmas Tree and at the foot of the Cross,
we thank You for making us whole. Keep us mindful that
the tree of Christmas has no meaning without the Tree of
Calvary.

Amen.

Holy Aubade

Satisfy us in the morning with Your steadfast love,
that we may rejoice and be glad all our days.
Psalm 90:14 (NIV)

All you angels and saints in Heaven,
All you mountains, oceans, streams deserts, valleys,
All you creatures of the oceans, the grassy plains, the skies,
All of mankind huddled in humanity,
　　Sing a greeting to the most holy dawn.
　　Sing a love song to the Dayspring on High Who has come o us.
　　Let all creatures raise a love song, a Holy Aubade, to welcome our Savior.
　　He Who was promised has come.
　　The Dayspring has divided human history. He brings the holy whiteness of forgiveness of sin. He brings the dawning of hope in the redemption of mankind.
　　He brings His steadfast love to Christmas morning.
　　Sing a Christmas song to the Babe of Bethlehem.
　　Sing rejoicing in the eternal purpose of this morning.
　　Sing a Holy Aubade.

Amen.

Bethlehem Intersection

Jesus, Journeying One,
Your Nativity approaches.
You travel through history towards our celebration of
Your birth.
You travel from eternity towards our Christmas.
You travel through our sins and sorrows, weakness of
will. You travel through our experiences, around our baggage
of foolish vain desires and inappropriate attempts at religion
to better know You.
We travel to You, to Bethlehem of Heart, through the
crush and press of holiday expectations.
We travel to You through time pressures to perform, to
render happiness of Christmas to our loved ones via plastic
presentations and pumped up praise.
Our junction is the Bethlehem Intersection where Your
eternal glory and generosity meet our ephemeral existence
In Your mercy, prevent us from taking a wrong turn,
from pulling off the heart highway to You, from parking
distractions and soul tanks on empty.
Bring us safely to the Christmas fullness of the
Bethlehem Intersection.
Thank You, Lord Jesus.

Amen.

Shepherd

And He will stand and feed His flock in the
strength of the Lord His God and they shall live secure.
Micah 5:4-5 (RSV)

May the Christmas Shepherd, the Good Shepherd, stand
in your life; stand tall above all the distractions and
discouragements of your everyday round.

May He who visits you at Christmas, the Eternal Bishop
of your soul, visit your heart and your holiday with new
revelations of His love for you as you reverence His Nativity.

May He feed you in the strength of the Lord His God
that you might live secure.

Secure in knowing you are loved.

Secure in your knowledge of Scripture.

Secure in your worship.

Secure in Holy Wisdom, especially for your loved ones.

Secure in your destination of eternity where the Good
Shepherd, now the Resurrected King, awaits your arrival
with joyful expectation.

May the Lord grant to you the Christmas gift of
answering each word of every prayer I have prayed for you,
dear one in the faith.

Amen.

Postlude Presence

And the Word became flesh and dwelt among us, full
of grace and truth; we have beheld His glory; glory as of the
only Son from the Father.

John 1:14(RSV)

Christmas Lord,

Bedraggled and dried Christmas trees in curbs along the
street, vagrant tinsel dangling from bare needles.

Bedraggled and dried up expectations, mis-directed
efforts at cheer, returning gifts, exhaustion, unmet needs.

Your birth still a mystery beyond our comprehension.

We pack away replicas of Your Manger in cardboard
boxes and place them on attic shelves.

But we cannot wrap Your message, box it and place it
out of sight until next Christmas.

You call to us from the Manger, from the Cross and
from Your Heavenly throne.

You remind us that as You dwelt among us in our
human flesh, You were and are full of grace and truth.

Come to us in the traditional Twelve Days of Christmas.

Mercifully grant to us the wisdom to keep Your Manger,
transformed from cardboard to conviction, foremost in our
lives and not on a shelf

Be Thou, O Christmas Lord, our Postlude Presence, a
reprise of grace echoing the prelude of Advent.

Amen.

Happy New Year

May you embrace the New Year as the new creation in Christ your are (2 Cor.5:17).

May you accept the new spirit He has placed within you and relinquish your heart of stone ((Jer. 31:31).

May you follow the new commandment to love, as He loves you, the people He has placed in your life (John 13:34).

May you remember each day that you have Jesus as a Heavenly Mediator of the new covenant of salvation (Heb 9:15).

May your daily alarm clock be an awareness that the Lord's mercies are new every morning (Lam 3:23).

May your heart be filled with new wine ((Matt 9:17).

May you worship with a new song (Ps 96:1).

May your mind allow the teaching of Jesus to have authority in Your life (Mk 1:27).

May you travel in joy towards the new heaven and the new earth ,the new Jerusalem where He waits for you (Rev 21:1).

May He, Who makes all things new, refresh every day of your year that it might be the Happiest of New Years(Rev 21:5).

Amen.

January First

You shall have no other gods before me.
Deuteronomy 5:7(NIV)

Dear one in the faith,
  May the Lord Jesus, the Alpha and the Omega,
  astonish you with the grace to embrace Him as the First.
  First before opinions, attitudes, perspectives,
relationships and responsibilities.
  First before the ephemeral enticements of the world.
  First before the adornment of self with glittering
godlessness .
  First before the dark temptations of your soul.
  First before the willfulness to be yourself first.
  First as each day begins.
  First before each word spoken.
  First before each gesture offered.
  First before each decision made.
  May you stand before Him, the Alpha and the Omega,
as a faithful servant on the last as on the first day of the New
Year.

Amen.

Christmas Basket

Gather the pieces that are left over. Let nothing be wasted.

John 6:12(NIV)

Blessed Lord Jesus,

In Your merciful economy of "nothing be wasted," help us to understand we are not wasted in the Kingdom. We left-overs from Your miraculous works need the assurance Your grace alone provides.

Grant to us the blessed insight to perceive our struggles, sins and sorrows as precious enough to be gathered. Bless our broken-ness with the strength to remain faithful fragments.

Grant to us the energy and the wisdom of witness to Your healing of the broken pieces of our lives.

Gather us in Your grace to be ever thankful the basket is Your heart, Jesus.

Amen.

About the Cover

Set a guard over my mouth, O Lord;
Keep watch over the door of my lips!
Psalm 141:3 (RSV)

The cover icon of The Holy Silence (© Christine Simoneau Hales) depicts the young boy Jesus.

It reminds us that Jesus knows and loves our inner child, the child summoned in our hearts at Christmas. It is the child He invited to come into the Kingdom, the child to whom the Kingdom belongs.

He also was once a child, as were we.

The dual nature of Christ's Divinity and humanity, being of the Heavenly realm as well as that of earth, appears as wings.

The Holy Silence bids us quiet our lips and our hearts and come to Him.

It blesses us with the knowledge we are loved beyond our imaginings.

May the reader enter into The Holy Silence and be blessed within the pages of this book of Christmas Prayers.

Amen.

A page reserved for the reader's own personal prayer for a Holy Christmas.

_____

_____

_____

_____

_____

_____

_____

_____

_____

_____

Christmas Prayers

Christmas Prayers

About the Author

Judith Hannemann has written "Christmas Prayers" as a gift for family and friends in the Body of Christ. It is a reminder of the greatest of all gifts in the birth of Jesus Christ. She has also written a collection of "Prayers" (AuthorHouse) as an encouragement to pray. Judith lives in Maine where she teaches English at the University of Southern Maine."

About the Cover Artist

Christine Simoneau Hales lives in the UK with her husband, the photographer Mick Hales. They have three children and are dedicated to bringing God's Kingdom here on earth. Her website is: www.halesart.com, or www.christinehales.com

Photo credit: Mick Hales